The Word Is Near You

Wycliffe Studies in Gospel, Church, and Culture

The series entitled Wycliffe College Studies in Gospel, Church, and Culture is intended to present topical subject matter in an accessible form and seeks to appeal to a broad audience. Typically titles in the series derive from sermons given by the faculty of Wycliffe College, Toronto, in its Founders' Chapel. The current volume is the fifth in the series.

Many thanks to the contributors to this current volume. I also want to thank Rachel Lott of Wycliffe College for her work on formatting the manuscript.

Peter M. B. Robinson

The Word Is Near You

Seeds of the Reformation

EDITED BY

Peter M. B. Robinson

WIPF & STOCK · Eugene, Oregon

THE WORD IS NEAR YOU
Seeds of the Reformation
Wycliffe Studies in Gospel, Church, and Culture

Wipf & Stock
An Imprint of Wipf and Stock Publishers
199 W. 8th Ave., Suite 3
Eugene, OR 97401

www.wipfandstock.com

PAPERBACK ISBN: 978-1-5326-5057-4
HARDCOVER ISBN: 978-1-5326-5058-1
EBOOK ISBN: 978-1-5326-5059-8

Manufactured in the U.S.A.

Contents

Introduction

PETER M. B. ROBINSON

"WHAT EXACTLY ARE WE celebrating?" That is a question which came up again and again during the celebration of the 500th anniversary of the Reformation. At times it seems as though the legacy of the Reformation is primarily one of division. In many cases division has been the rule rather than the exception: new denominations form only to quickly divide again. Having divided over one issue, it is much easier to then divide over another. Not exactly the kind of legacy the reformers envisioned.

There are signs that we are moving in a somewhat different direction today—towards a different kind of denominational fluidity with denominational distinctions appearing to matter less and less. New students arriving every September at Wycliffe College come from a wide variety of denominations, with the majority having changed denominations at least once if not several times. This denominational dance is both positive and negative: positive in that it suggests people are more open to engaging with other Christians in spite of denominational differences, and negative because, at least in part, it seems to reflect a consumer approach to church in which we are free to pick and choose the denomination which works best "for me."

Living in the midst of a divided church, it can be important to recognize that the reformers, at least initially, had no intention of leaving the church or encouraging division. Rather, their hope and intention was to challenge the church to turn back in faithfulness to God. That call to faithfulness is a reminder that we need to hear again today. The difficulty is that not many would look to the reformers or seek to learn from them, because they can seem distant or even alien to us today, far more distant than some current leaders in the Catholic Church, particularly when the pope is a man like Francis. Martin Luther, John Calvin, and Thomas Cranmer, for example, are not only foreign to our modern sensibilities, but there are elements of their writing or their actions which seem abhorrent to us today. As a result many in the church, even in the Protestant Church, find it all too easy to dismiss or ignore their witness.

We live in an era where it has been far too easy to dismiss the past, especially when there are elements that we do not understand or that we disagree with. At the same time, beginning in the early 20th century, there has been a significant shift in the appreciation of both Eastern Orthodoxy and Catholicism and a recognition that those of us in the Protestant Church have much to learn from them. In an article to celebrate the 500th anniversary of the Reformation, Stanley Hauerwas posed the question, "Why am I not Catholic?" He goes on to note that Catholicism is "an intellectually rich theological tradition better able to negotiate the acids of our culture."[1] Indeed, some of the issues which concerned the reformers are just as much a problem in Protestant churches today as they were in

1. Hauerwas, "The Reformation is Over."

the Catholic Church then. We have questions concerning faith, the way we are to think about and engage with the Bible, basic questions about the church, its identity and authority, as well as questions concerning the person and work of Christ.

In the midst of the decline of the church in the Western world, it is often asked what will this next era bring? Not only do we have a lot to learn from other denominations, we have a lot to learn from our respective and our shared traditions—from Irenaeus to Thomas Aquinas to Gregory of Palamas to Martin Luther. Several recent commentators describe a theology of retrieval or *ressourcement*: an ecumenical endeavor broadly shared across the church from Roman Catholic to Eastern Orthodox, as well as many Protestant denominations, as we seek to recover something of the wisdom of the saints. Disillusioned by the empty promise of steady progress towards an enlightened future and uncomfortably aware of the naïve optimism of our own era, there has been a growing recognition of how much we have to learn from a careful reading of and engagement with the tradition. Consistently, this retrieval has been driven not by historical curiosity or by a desire to better understand the past but by a commitment to see renewal in the church today—a call to faithfulness. A key element in this retrieval has been the desire to understand how Scripture has been read, appreciated, and responded to, not primarily as a historical artifact but as God's gift in and to the church as it is extended over time and space. God continues to work through his church in the midst of her divisions and her wandering—even through her divisions and wanderings.

That brings us to this collection of essays which were first presented as a faculty sermon series at Wycliffe

College. These essays begin to explore many of the concerns which shaped the Reformation while acknowledging some of its strengths and weaknesses. They do this through engaging with select scriptures which were of particular importance during the Reformation. There are compelling reasons to look carefully to the reformers and how the reformers read the Bible in the desire to help renew the church in the present. There are two reasons in particular which I would like to mention. First, as we have already suggested, listening carefully to how other Christians read or have read the biblical text gives us more breadth in our own reading and understanding, while serving to unmask some of the presuppositions or assumptions we may not even be aware of. Paying careful attention to the broader tradition protects us from a romanticism in our own understanding and counters the tendency to pick and choose those elements of tradition that appeal to us. Secondly, in one way or another in the West we are all children of the Reformation, and we need to know who we are. The writing and thinking of the reformers has not only shaped the church, it has shaped the values and structures of the world that we live in. For good and for ill, our identity has been formed by the Reformation. Paying careful attention to the reformers allows us to "own" who we are, where we come from, and to discern what has shaped our values, desires, and lives, all while learning to listen more carefully to God.

One thing is certain: we will benefit greatly from remembering our past, understanding how we have been formed, and most particularly seeking to be alert to the ways in which God has been and is at work in his Church and in the world.

1

The Heart Wants What It Wants

Joseph Mangina

"The heart wants what it wants. There's no logic to these things. You meet someone and you fall in love and that's that."

That's the great comedian and filmmaker Woody Allen, explaining how it was that he abandoned his wife Mia Farrow to take up with Farrow's adoptive daughter Soon-Yi Previn, whom he married in 1997. Allen is a very well-read man, so it's possible that when he said that, he was consciously or unconsciously channeling Emily Dickinson. In a letter to a friend written in 1862, Dickinson wrote, "The heart wants what it wants, or else it does not care."

"The heart wants what it wants." On the lips of Woody Allen, the words sound like a justification: human desire is mysterious, we are its helpless playthings. Don't blame me, blame my heart. From the pen of Emily Dickinson the words sound more like a comment on how the heart, desire, *eros*, is close to the animating principle of what it means to be human. The heart wants what it wants, or else it does not care. The heart desires, or else we die. Human beings are lovers down to the very core. It is a deeply Augustinian insight: "You have made us for yourself," writes Augustine on the very first page of the *Confessions*, "and our hearts are restless until they find their rest in you." So likewise Pascal tells us that "the heart has its reasons, of which reason knows nothing."

The problem, of course, is that the heart often wants the wrong things. The heart wants what *it* wants. Not what is good, or courageous, or true, or of assistance to the neighbor, but that which feeds the fantasies of our desires. So we read in Genesis: "And God saw that the wickedness of man was great in the earth, and that every imagination of the thoughts of his heart was only evil continually" (Gen 6:5, KJV). The twentieth-century novelist and philosopher Iris Murdoch spoke of the "fat, relentless ego" and showed the human wreckage it causes in her dark, funny, and weird novels. The fat relentless ego: a good description of the human condition. We Christians have another name for the heart's evil imagining. We call it sin.

The Old Testament is ruthlessly honest about sin's empire, the way it plants its flag not just in the Gentile nations with their idols and abominable practices—that is only to be expected—but in the midst of the covenant between God and Israel. Israel, God's own beloved people, have sinned. They have dishonored the Torah and broken the covenant. They have answered God's love with malice and injustice. The situation is dire. What is needed is not good intentions or promises to do better next time, or any other sort of halfway measure, but a radical new beginning: a new love, a new affection, a new obedience. We encounter this vision of the future in many parts of the Old Testament, but perhaps nowhere more powerfully than in Jeremiah 31:33–34:

> But this is the covenant that I will make with the
> house of Israel after those days, says the LORD:
> I will put my law within them, and I will write
> it on their hearts; and I will be their God, and
> they shall be my people. No longer shall they
> teach one another, or say to each other, "Know
> the LORD," for they shall all know me, from the
> least of them to the greatest, says the LORD; for
> I will forgive their iniquity, and remember their
> sin no more.

The covenant established on Sinai pointed the way, offered a vision of human life as it should be, showed what it might look like to live in peace with God and one's neighbor, to be one of the "quiet in the land." This Godward shaping of human existence is what the Ten Commandments are all about. But in the new covenant of which Jeremiah speaks, obedience will come from within; it will be written on the human heart. The heart will indeed want what it wants, and what it wants will be *good*.

This series is about the Reformation of the sixteenth century, and maybe you were wondering when I would get around to talking about that. But you see, I already have. For notice something about the Jeremiah passage: it is in the form of a *promise*. There is no more reformational category than that. Protestant theologians from Luther to Barth to Robert Jenson have read Scripture as one long record of God's promise-making and promise-keeping. Jeremiah's words were addressed to the Israel of his own day, teetering on the brink of exile. But they gesture forward to the day when God's promises to Israel, to the nations, and to the whole world would be fulfilled in the sending of God's own Son and the pouring out of the Spirit upon all flesh. The new covenant envisioned by Jeremiah is none other than the New Testament of our Lord and Savior Jesus

Christ. It is simply the gospel—the glad tidings that God has visited his people, not just to forgive sin or usher in the kingdom but to transform our hearts. There is no more profoundly reformational theme than that. The law in its unity with the gospel, the gospel as the true meaning of the law, the Spirit as the divine person who writes that law in our hearts so that we may love the Lord our God with all our heart, and with all our soul, and with all our strength; and our neighbors as ourselves. This is the gift God has given us in Jesus, who is—as Hebrews tells us—the mediator of a new covenant, sealed with his own sprinkled blood.

If we had more time, we could play with this theme as it is discussed by John Calvin in his *Institutes*. Calvin wrote eloquently about the unity between the old and new covenants, despite their very real differences. Or we might explore how Karl Barth, in his doctrine of election, saw Jesus Christ himself as the eternal covenant of grace uniting God and humankind. But we do not have time in this brief reflection. So I will instead leave you with an image, drawn not from Calvin but from Luther. Luther's personal seal consisted of a black cross on a red heart, resting on a white rose, the whole set against a field of blue and surrounded by a golden ring. The cross is black (Luther explains) because it puts to death our sin; the heart is red—its natural color—because the cross does not kill us but makes us alive; it perfects rather than destroys our nature. The white rose is the peace that comes to us through the gospel, while the blue field represents the joy that awaits us in heaven. The gold ring, finally, is the heavenly blessedness that lasts forever and has no end.

The heart wants what it wants. And in Christ our Lord, God has given us our heart's desire. May we take this gospel message out into the world that God has made, loved, and reconciled in the person of his beloved Son—to whom, with the Father and the Holy Spirit, be glory forever and ever.

Scripture: Jeremiah 31:31–34

Questions

1. What does it mean to say that the heart "is close to the animating principle of what it is to be human," or that human beings are "lovers down to the very core"? How much control do we have over what we love?

2. What is meant here by "old covenant" and "new covenant"? How are these covenants similar, and how are they different?

3. Why is the category of *promise* so important to our reading of the Bible? Why was it especially attractive to the Protestant reformers of the sixteenth century?

2

By Faith Alone

But What Exactly is Faith?

JUDY PAULSEN

THIS YEAR, AROUND THE world and across many denominations, the 500th anniversary of the Reformation is being recognized. For those of us studying or teaching theology, this is significant because we know how profoundly the Reformation affected the church. But how would you explain what was at the heart of the Reformation to someone who hadn't studied it?

One approach might be to start with what are sometimes called the "five solas": five short Latin phrases that emerged to summarize the reformers' theological convictions about the essentials of Christianity.

1. Sola Scriptura ("Scripture alone"): The Scriptures alone are our highest authority.

2. Sola Gratia ("grace alone"): We are saved by the grace of God alone.

3. Solus Christus ("Christ alone"): Jesus Christ alone is our Lord, Savior, and King.

4. Soli Deo Gloria ("to the glory of God alone"): We live for the glory of God alone.

5. Sola Fide ("faith alone"): We are saved through faith alone in Jesus Christ.

The third chapter of Romans, like so much of Paul's letter to the Romans, speaks about faith. What exactly *is* this thing called faith and what difference does it make? We live in a culture in which "faith" means to many people something between *dogged positivity* and *wishful thinking*. It is often seen as a feeling: *rooted in the self, manufactured by the self,* and *useful (or harmful) to the self.* Faith as it is described in Scripture, and so as understood by the reformers, is something far more substantive.

In the letter to the Romans alone faith is described as the root of obedience (Rom 1:5), an instrument of justification (Rom 3:30), and the pathway to righteousness (Rom 4:13).

Luther described faith this way:

> Faith is a work of God in us, which changes us and brings us to birth anew from God (cf. John 1). It kills the old Adam, makes us completely different people in heart, mind, senses, and all our powers, and brings the Holy Spirit with it. What a living, creative, active powerful thing is faith! It is impossible that faith ever stop doing good. Faith doesn't ask whether good works are to be done, but, before it is asked, it has done them. It is always active.[1]

1. *Preface to the Letter of St. Paul to the Romans*, 2:2254–68.

Far from seeing faith as a feeling rooted in, manufactured by, and useful to the self, the reformers saw it as a trust *in* the work *of* Christ, enlivened *by* the Holy Spirit, and bringing about righteousness *for* the glory of God. Certainly they recognized faith is a *human response*. But rather than a dogged positivity manufactured by the self, the reformers saw faith as a humble confidence in *God's* presence, power and grace, whether in times of ease or hardship.

Now, for sure, people do experience faith in times of ease. When we're out in the beauty of nature and we're seized with awe and wonder at God's creative power. When we've read or heard something profound that has moved us to a new level of understanding and action. When during worship we have a powerful sense of God's healing, convicting, loving presence.

But, as lovely as such experiences are, surely these can only be the shallowest form of faith, for they lean heavily on our *natural* responses. A *deeper* faith in God is that which *defies* natural surroundings, thoughts, or feelings. As any pastor or parish priest can tell you, faith is a hope that wells up *even when* someone has been devastated by a son's suicide, or they find themselves sorting through the rubble of their flooded home, or gasping for their last breath, or staring into the face of some serious moral failure.

Faith is an assurance that exists in spite of any natural response. It is a hope and conviction that a new and much better reality is already on the way and that we can live into *that* reality in the here and now. As Hebrews 11:1 says, "Faith is the assurance of things hoped for, the conviction of things not seen."

Faith whispers the most amazing things in the direst of circumstances. When you're *not* in the beauty of nature, or belting out your favorite hymn, but are losing your eyesight and are stuck alone and in a wheelchair in some miserable nursing home. It is *then* that faith will say, "You are nonetheless advancing toward a glory that will exceed all other glories known or unknown." Or, when you honestly admit those private thoughts that you wouldn't want anyone else to know about, the ones that reveal the true depth of your character flaws, it is *then* that faith says, "These are nonetheless giving way to Christ-likeness because God is at work in you, bringing you to new life."

Paul writes to the Romans, "A righteousness apart from law has been made known." But let's be clear, this righteousness extends beyond us as individuals. Faith says that the *condition* of sin, endemic to the human condition, has already been dealt its death blow. The chains have already dropped off, and people who have lived their whole lives as slaves to sin are now learning to live into a new identity as children of God and brothers and sisters of Christ. Faith stirs people around the world to *act* for a kingdom of justice, peace, and mercy—a kingdom that, while yet to be fully realized, is on its way. It is faith that lets us croak out together, "This is my Father's world, O let me ne'er forget that though the wrong seems oft so strong He is the ruler yet."

But how does one grow in Christian faith and the righteousness it brings? For the reformers, knowing the story of God's gracious saving work in the Lord Jesus, as revealed throughout the entirety of the Bible, was key. Paul wrote, " . . . a righteousness apart from the law has been made known, *to which the Law and the Prophets testify.*" For it is the story of the "one and only God who will justify the circumcised by faith and the uncircumcised by that same faith." Sola Scriptura and Sola Fide are inextricably linked.

Faith. It is not a dogged positivity or wishful thinking rooted in the self. It is an assurance enlivened by the Spirit in what has already been accomplished by God through Christ our Lord and what is witnessed to throughout the Scriptures. To those who have never heard the gospel, faith means so little. To Christians, it means so much. Let that alone be enough reason to share what we've come to know. Thanks be to God!

Scripture: Romans 3:21–24 and 27–29

Questions

1. What are the stories or passages of Scripture that have most formed you in the faith?

2. Describe a time of struggle during which faith brought comfort, discernment, or hope. What did you learn during this time?

3. Describe a time of ease during which you were especially aware of God's presence. How did you change as a result?

4. What behaviors or characteristics have changed in you as you've grown in faith?

3

The Devil and the Details

TERENCE DONALDSON

IT'S AN EXPERIENCE THAT happens from time to time for readers of Scripture. You are reading a familiar passage, something you know almost by heart, and suddenly you notice that something is missing. An aspect of the text, a detail of some kind, something you thought was an integral part of the passage, simply isn't there. You read the passage again, and every place you look for it, it keeps on not being there.

I had a memorable experience of this kind quite a while ago when I was studying mountain scenes and mountain imagery in the Gospels. Ever since I was a child I had sung hymns with lines such as "There is a green hill far away" or "free to all a healing stream flows from Calvary's mountain." Along with Mount Sinai and Mount Zion, "Mount Calvary" had been a fixture of my spiritual geography from the beginning. So I reread the crucifixion accounts in the four Gospels, fully expecting to find some indication that Christ's crucifixion had taken place on a mountain, or at least on a hill of some kind. I looked for it, but there it wasn't. To be sure, as I looked further I was able to discover why this interpretation emerged, and how it eventually became such a fixed element in Christian tradition that it was woven back into our reading of the Gospel accounts themselves. I don't have time to say much more about this development here, though it does connect in a significant way with the third chapter of Genesis—a passage that represents another instance of the same phenomenon.

In the third chapter of Genesis the detail that just keeps on not being there is the figure of Satan himself. The story of what Christians came to describe as the Fall is deeply embedded in Christian tradition and in the narrative framework within which we read Scripture. And in this story, Satan plays a central role. A fallen angel and now the arch-enemy of God, Satan is determined to thwart God's purposes in the newly created world and the place of human beings within it. And so he disguises himself as a serpent, unsettles Eve's simple trust in God's word, beguiles her into eating the forbidden fruit along with Adam, and thus succeeds in plunging the human race and the whole created order into a morass of sin, guilt, punishment, and death. (To return to the thread left dangling a moment ago, in a subplot to this story, the site of Adam's burial was a mountain, a mountain that later also served as the site of the crucifixion of Christ, the new Adam.)

Our focus here is verse fifteen, part of the climactic confrontation scene in which God calls all three characters to account. Here God has this to say to the serpent: "I will put enmity between you and the woman, and between your seed and hers; he will strike your head and you will strike his heel." In the context of the more developed story of the Fall, this verse is read as a preliminary announcement of the gospel. The "seed" of the woman is taken to be Christ, and the blow to the head of the serpent is taken to refer to the crushing defeat that would be administered to Satan and his evil host through Christ's death and resurrection.

It is a grand and magnificent story, told with compelling force in classic works such as Milton's *Paradise Lost* and Michelangelo's Sistine Chapel, and deeply embedded in Christian consciousness through the countless retellings in mystery plays, stained glass windows, sermons, commentaries, Sunday School lessons, and so on, down through the centuries. So much so that when we read the bare words of the passage, it's the whole grand narrative that takes shape in our mind, just as some people hear the strains of Handel's *Messiah* as they read some passages in Isaiah.

But when we focus our attention on the bare words of the passage, a lot of this falls away. The adversary appears simply as one of the field animals that God created—the craftiest, to be sure, but without a hint of anything more. The judgment seems to be more a matter of ongoing mutual enmity than of any decisive victory of one over the other. And Satan is nowhere to be seen; the devil is certainly not in the details. Is this just one of those times, then, when a serpent is just a serpent? Is this just a curious story about a talking snake?

Well, hardly. The story, after all, deals with fundamental and perennial human issues: the knowledge of good and evil, life and death, mortality and immortality, God's commandments and human disobedience, sexuality and marriage, childbirth and lines of descent, toil, pain, and suffering. Further, unlike the story of Balaam's talking donkey, tucked away in some obscure spot in the book of Numbers, this story stands at the head of the canon and deals with the progenitors of the whole human race. The story, then, is hard to ignore. The issues it touches on are part of the warp and woof of human existence, as each of us knows all too well. And so, in the ongoing experience of God's people, as the perception of God's purposes in human history developed, as awareness of the powers of evil became more pressing, and as the hope of final redemption came more clearly into view, it is not surprising that faithful readers would return to this passage and wrestle with it in light of the unfolding story of God, Israel, and humankind.

To be sure, in the rest of Israel's scriptures, there is very little interest in the story of Adam and Eve in the garden. Adam is mentioned only a small handful of times, and Eve not at all. In the period leading up to the time of Jesus, however, Jewish interpreters begin to pay more attention to the passage. Curiously enough, one thing that caught their attention was the ability of the serpent to talk. Both Josephus's *Antiquities* and the book of *Jubilees* contain the little detail that all of the animals in the Garden of Eden could speak (in Hebrew, according to *Jubilees*), but then they lost the ability as a result of the serpent's action. More important for our purposes, though, is the fact that Jewish interpreters became increasingly interested in the figure of Satan and the story of Adam and Eve, and many of the elements that appear in the full-blown Christian story are found already in Jewish interpretation of Scripture. While the full-blown story emerges only in the second century, several of the elements are found in the New Testament as well, probably informed by Jewish exegesis. I'm thinking here, for example, of Revelation 12:9, which speaks of "that ancient serpent, who is called the Devil and Satan, the deceiver of the whole world," or Romans 16:20, where

Paul tells his readers that "the God of peace will shortly crush Satan under your feet."

We are interested in this passage because of its place in the Protestant Reformation and its importance for the reformers. I think it's fair to say that, while the reformers took issue with some of the more recent Roman Catholic interpretation, for the most part they simply carried over the interpretation of Genesis 3:15 that had developed in the early centuries of the church. But there is one aspect of Calvin's interpretation that caught my attention and that I want to mention. If this essay has an element of exhortation and edification, here it is.

In the traditional interpretation of the verse, the reference to the "seed" of the woman was taken as a straightforward reference to Christ and thus to his definitive triumph over Satan and the powers of sin and death. While Calvin says that he would be happy with this interpretation, he feels that it does too much violence to the plain sense of the text. As we have already noted, the verse seems to speak not of a single decisive victory but of an ongoing struggle, and not of a single descendant but of a whole line of descendants. Of course, says Calvin, we who live after the coming of Christ can be assured of the final victory over sin and death because of Christ's death and resurrection. But he reads the verse as placing the emphasis elsewhere. First, the emphasis is on the idea that both the ongoing struggle and the ultimate victory are centered on the human race itself. And second, the victory is not yet complete; the struggle with the powers of sin and death continues. While I don't think Calvin was familiar with Jewish exegesis, it is worth noting that his reading is similar to the one that appears in the Targum Pseudo-Jonathan on this verse—except that in Calvin's reading it is Christ, rather than the Torah, that gives people the ability to tread on the head of the serpent and to resist the powers of sin and death.

This, I think, places the emphasis where it should be. The forces of evil and the death-dealing powers of sin are too evident and too pervasive for the church to retreat into any triumphalistic and self-serving form of the gospel. While victory is assured, we are called to engage faithfully in the ongoing struggle and to look ahead to a victory in which the human race itself, with Christ at its head, is a full participant.

Scripture: Genesis 3:8–15

Questions

1. Compare Paul's summary of the Garden of Eden story in Romans 5:12 ("Therefore, just as sin came into the world through one man, and death through sin . . . ") with the story as it is found in Genesis 3 and in later interpretations of the passage (i.e., in which the serpent is identified as Satan). What strikes you about the similarities and differences?

2. Do you think that Gen 3:15 speaks more of a decisive one-time crushing of the serpent by a single descendant of the woman, or of an ongoing hostility between two groups of descendants? Note that the word translated as "offspring" in Gen 3:15 [NRSV; literally, "seed"] is elsewhere translated as "descendants" [e.g., Gen 9:9; 12:7; 15:5]. Note also that the subject of the verb "strike" (first occurrence) could refer back to "offspring."

3. If we read the verse as having to do with an ongoing conflict between the powers of sin and the human race, what form does this conflict take in our own day? In our own lives?

4

The Law Too Is Gracious

EPHRAIM RADNER

"WHEREFORE THE LAW [IS] holy, and the commandment holy, and just, and good" (Rom 7:12), and Christ its "telos" (Rom 10:4). These words of Paul from Romans are arguably among the most fertile in the New Testament, and their engagement continues to spur some of the most creative theological endeavor in the church. To which we might add Jesus' own words, that he came "not to abolish the law, but to make it full" (Matt 5:17).

We are used to thinking of Luther's stark opposition between Law and Gospel—which he took up from Paul, after all—as definitive of the Reformation's initiating energies. "The Gospel gives freely," he wrote, "but the Law exacts impossible things from us."[1] But in fact, Protestants—Luther included in his own way—sought continually to bridge this simple opposition by seeing how the law was lodged *within* grace; and, from their side, over the past centuries, Catholics have done the same, seeing how grace is lodged within the law. You would think that, by 2017, there would be some kind of common ground here, and

1. Luther, *Galatians*, 126.

there *has* been among some theologians. But philosophical liberalism has culturally triumphed, and that philosophy insists that religion itself is a form of deadly legalism. So the opposition between Law and Gospel is now part of our inescapable social baggage. We are all weighed down by it. Beware!

Yet, as I just noted, the Reformation's vital tradition was always engaged in figuring out how the law might be lodged within divine grace itself. Every Protestant church pursued this question in its own way. The Decalogue—that is, the Ten Words of God, the Ten Commandments—were at the heart of this common pursuit; and the Decalogue is thus a central Reformation scriptural text. It is a key part of every Reformation catechism—Lutheran, Calvinist, and so on. Though, to be sure, it is also a key part of every *Catholic* catechism. Every Christian, until recently, of any tradition, was taught as the foundation of their faith the Decalogue, the Apostles' Creed, and the Lord's Prayer. Every one. More than any text from Romans or Galatians, Protestant Christians knew the Ten Commandments. It was part of the baptismal covenant itself.

There were differences among the churches in how they engaged the Decalogue foundationally. Perhaps the most integrated approach was that of the English reformers, with Thomas Cranmer in the lead. When Cranmer had a free hand to revise the English liturgy, in the 1552 Book of Common Prayer (BCP), he added the Decalogue to the Communion Service. It was a unique innovation. Although the German-French reformer Martin Bucer may have suggested it to Cranmer, no other Reformed liturgy followed suit.

And nobody quite knows why Cranmer did it. Yet there it is, still in the present-day BCP Communion service, right after the opening Collect: the priest, "facing the people" (who are kneeling), says, "Hear the Law of God which was given to Israel in old time. God spake these words and said . . . ," and then the priest "rehearses" each commandment. And after each commandment is spoken, the people pray, "Lord, have mercy upon us, and incline our hearts to keep this law." And finally, after the last commandment is proclaimed—"Thou shalt not covet they neighbor's house, thou shalt not covet thy neighbor's wife, nor his servant, nor his maid, nor his ox, nor his ass, nor any thing that is his"—the people pray, "Lord, have mercy upon us, and write all these thy laws in our hearts, we beseech thee."

This too is the Reformation. And there are at least four key things to say about the particularly Reformation meaning of this practice. First, coming at the beginning of worship, most commentators viewed the rehearsal of the Decalogue as a necessary presentation of the holiness and awesome sovereignty of the creating God, before whom our lives are given over in Christ. "Lord have mercy upon us," we say, with a clear sense that we can approach God only through his forgiveness of our violation of his sanctity and will. And to do this, we have need for the very life of God at work in us. "Incline our hearts to keep this law," we cry out in yearning and submission. The eighteenth-century divine Charles Wheatly speaks of the priest standing and proclaiming the laws, not in his own person, but as the voice of God, speaking through Moses again from the mountain, before a great calling and future that lies before Israel and now before the gathered Christian congregation. We are being readied for a tremendous journey.

Secondly, the people pray at the end of the Decalogue's pronouncement, "write all these thy laws in our hearts."

The move here is twofold. First, God is at work personally in *offering* these commands to us. In this sense, they are the "gift" of God even in Luther's sense. Write them for us! Give them to us! Exodus 31:18 tells us that the tablets were inscribed by the very "finger of God." The God who creates is the God who gives us the law. Second, this is a mark of incredible condescension and divine involvement in our lives. No wonder that the giving of the Torah was viewed by Jews often in a manner similar to the second chapter of Philippians: the giving of the law *is* God "coming down" and dwelling among us.

But if so, how? The answer is: "In Christ"! And that brings us to the third thing we need to say: the law is *always* "given" "in Christ," who is personally the Mount Sinai in its revelatory gifts. Hence, the prayer the people make, "write all these thy laws in our hearts," is a clear reference to the first Reformation text we heard in this series, Jeremiah 31:31: "I will put my law within them, and I will write it upon their hearts; and I will be their God, and they shall be my people." Anglicans were clear that the commandments were themselves re-given to us as a divine vocation by Jesus himself. "If you would enter life, keep the commandments," he says to the inquirer after salvation in Matthew 19:17. But more than that, they were given "in Christ," in his Spirit, working among us, inscribing them, fulfilling them, moving us to keep them.

Finally, the "us" is important, as in the words of Jeremiah: "I will be their God and they will be my people." The Decalogue is a "corporate" or communal gift. If given in Christ, in his Spirit, the law here takes its form in the body of Christ, the church, directly. The law is the "grace" of the body, the humbling gift of a God awesomely sovereign and holy, to grant life to Adam, the human being, the human race, now taken up in Christ as his church.

Although Luther's Law-Gospel tension, or even conflict, shaped the thinking of certain early English reformers, a deeper English tradition soon asserted itself anew: there is grace in the law. Grace is always fundamental, and justification is given by grace. But the law itself is a gift, and it is a powerful gift when embraced in Christ Jesus. How exactly? On the one hand, by his accompaniment in our obedience, even his fulfilment of it for our incapable hearts. On the other, this leading finds its palpable fulfillment in terms of corporate love, that is, the ordering of a social body in mutual service.

The sense that in the Decalogue we are shown how God and neighbor are properly served by the grace of Christ is a peculiar English Protestant sentiment: that is, we are Christians only insofar as we are reborn in service of a "commonwealth"; and that commonwealth is truthful and good only insofar as it is centered in God's life. We pray the Decalogue because divine grace comes to us always in the form of an ordered social life of mutual charity. There is no love without such order; there is no ordered social life—human life, that is—without such charity.

This is all a very important challenge to contemporary assumptions. "Thou shalt have none other gods but me . . . thou shalt not bow down to them . . . I am a jealous God . . . thou shalt not take the name of the Lord thy God in vain . . . keep holy the Sabbath day . . . honour thy mother and father . . . thou shalt do no murder, nor adultery, nor stealing, nor false witness against thy neighbor . . . thou shalt not covet . . . " These actually sum up some of the great Reformation commitments, once so dear, though now mostly forgotten: God's life above all else, against all self-centeredness, idolatry, blasphemy, distraction; the incredibly intense and focused Protestant concerns with God's holiness, with prayer, with dedicated reading of the Scriptures, with an ordered life given over to the purity of God's Spirit. And then, the deep commitment to the order of a common life—family and parents, the restraint of violence, material modesty and generosity, the protection of the weak (the poor, women, children), absolute integrity of demeanor and communication. To receive *this*? To be empowered in its embrace? To know the mercy of God in Christ in pursuing its ordering energies? This is pure gift, pure grace.

Yet much of it has disappeared in our modern world, with its competitive and individual self-assertions and identity groups. It has disappeared even in our churches, I'm afraid, where frankly, the same competitive self-assertions prevail, where law and grace are pitted against each other in a false zero-sum game.

By contrast, the Decalogue stands, as it has always stood, as a great antidote to this quite natural slide into the abrasive forms of naturalism itself. The reformers deserve our attention for recognizing this gift, one we should receive with ever renewed thanksgiving and performance. God spake these words and said . . . Do these, sell your goods, and then come, follow me! (Matt 19:21).

Scripture: Exodus 20:1–17

Questions

1. We seem to find it very difficult to hold law and grace together in tension. At certain points in the history of the church, we have emphasized the law as primary.

More recently, a particular emphasis on grace appears to leave no room for the law at all. How does our inability to hold law and grace together shape our understanding of the Christian life today?

2. What does it mean to say that Christ is the telos or fulfillment of the law?

3. How can we together cultivate a sense of the law as a gift, rather than a barrier, to our knowing God and our living together as the people of God? How might we, with the reformers, learn to find the place for the law within grace?

5

I Am Not Ashamed

L. Ann Jervis

"For I am not ashamed of the *euangelion*; for in it the *dunamis theou* is for salvation for all who believe, to the Jew first and also the Greek. For *dikaiosune theou apokaluptetai*, from faith for faith. Just as it is written: the righteous out of faith *zesetai*" (Rom 1:16–17).

FOR A COUPLE OF reasons, I am reciting some parts of Paul's sentences in Greek. First, because this is a series on the Reformation, and one of the energies that propelled the most significant of the reformers was reading and studying the Bible in its original languages. And second because these verses may be very familiar to you. By leaving some of the more familiar parts in the Greek, I hope to help us hear them again for the first time.

Euangelion—gospel, which is the *dunamis theou*—power of God, for salvation for all, though to the Jew first. In the *euangelion* the *dikaiosune theou*—the righteousness of God—is *apokaluptetai*—revealed, unveiled, disclosed. From faith for faith, as it is written, the righteous out of faith *zesetai*—shall live.

These are dangerous words. And so Paul introduces them with "for I am not ashamed." This is not only a negative way of saying a positive thing; it is also an acknowledgement that there is immense and unavoidable potency in what he claims. The gospel as Paul presents it will necessarily provoke a strong reaction.

And the danger of these words has been evident during the 500 years since Luther first heard them afresh. These words are dangerous because they proclaim the clash between life and death, between sin and faith—a clash that is not just in the concepts these words describe, but in the reality of our world. Paul knew, as did the reformers, as do we, that Death and Sin still stalk our world and our hearts. And that the power of God, the righteousness of God revealed in the gospel, is the only power that defeats God's enemies—Death and Sin. These words are dangerous to Death and Sin, and as we believe them, trust them, they put us in danger as well. We believers become the site of the struggle between life and death, between faith and sin. And, as the legacy of the Reformation shows, too often God's enemies have intimidated or deluded us.

In his commentary on Romans, the great Reformed thinker of the 20th century, Karl Barth, using the language of his time, described the depth of our capacity for delusion. "Men fall a prey first to themselves and then to the 'No-God' . . . Men obscure the distance between God and man . . . Thinking of ourselves what can be thought only of God, we are unable to think Him more highly than we think of ourselves. Being to ourselves what God ought to be to us, He is no more to us than we are to ourselves. This secret identification of ourselves with God carries with it our isolation from Him . . . Men have imprisoned and en-cased the truth—the righteousness of God."[1]

Reformed thinkers have written volumes and vol-umes on every word and phrase of Romans 1:16–17. And not only because what Paul says is so intellectually hori-zon breaking, but because Paul's claims about the gospel reveal salvation. They are life-giving. Luther commented on Romans 1:17: "human teachers set forth and inculcate the righteousness of people, that is, who is righteous, or how a person becomes righteous both in their own eyes and those of others. Only the gospel reveals the righteous-ness of God, that is, who is righteous and how a person becomes righteous before God, namely, alone by faith, which trusts the Word of God."[2] This was, as we all know, marvelous good news to Luther the Augustinian monk who had struggled mightily with whether or not he was righteous enough to please a righteous God. Luther heard Paul's words as liberation from this struggle: because he believed, he was righteous, and so he would live. God's righteousness was not a standard he had to strive with all his might to meet, but a gift to him. God's righteousness is an alien righteousness that allowed him, while still be-ing a sinner, also to be righteous—*simul justus et peccator*. *Dikaiosune theou* was not a burden which threatened him with death, it was a gift that gave him life.

The important mid-20th-century Lutheran commen-tator on Paul—E. Käsemann—underscored the *dunamis theou* nature of the gospel.[3] The gospel as God's power makes present now eternal life. Those in the Reformed tradition influenced by Käsemann and Barth have empha-

---

1. Barth, *Epistle to the Romans*, 44–45.

2. Luther, *Commentary on Romans*, 41.

3. Käsemann, *Commentary on Romans*, 24.

sized the apocalyptic nature of God's power in the gospel. J. L. Martyn and Beverly Roberts Gaventa hear Paul to be claiming that God has invaded the present evil age and is waging war on God's enemies—Sin and Death.[4] These are dangerous ideas. They cut so to the heart of our hearts and to the heart of reality that God's enemies do all that they can to twist them or blind us to them. This is what John Wesley saw had happened in the Protestant church. Christians had become complacent: "I believe, I am saved. So what." In this complacency Wesley saw Sin and Death distorting the truth of Paul's words. Through the Spirit, Wesley rekindled in the church a sense of the gospel as God's power for salvation. Individuals who have faith are freed to live for holiness and dedicate themselves to works of love.

In recent years, the church has been called to hear that these words are not only about the interior lives of individuals but that *dikaiosune theou*—the righteousness of God—is also the justice of God. There is so much more to say. I could talk about how the phrase "from faith" has been fruitfully interpreted as referring to Christ's faithfulness. I could talk about the many fertile ways that the *dikaiosune theou* has been understood, ways that allow us to wash the word clean again and hear it as referring to all that we actually long for—life without destruction, violence, displaced peoples, the threat of nuclear war, the torments in our souls caused by our conflicting desires or our lack of wisdom. Righteousness—everything being all right, as good and as pure and as beautiful and as trustworthy and as faithful as God. In the gospel, God is revealing God's justice for all that God has made—human and

4. Martyn, *Galatians* and *Theological Issues in the Letters of Paul*. Gaventa, "The Cosmic Power of Sin," 229–40.

non-human. And believers are called to see God's justice and work along with it.

I can only exhort myself and you to recognize how dangerous these words are—dangerous to the pseudo-reality in which we live—the illusion that we can make our lives up on our own; the illusion that we can produce justice apart from God; the illusion that life is ours to create; that human power is the greatest power; that if God exists, God is removed and uninvolved in human affairs and the groaning of creation. Because these words proclaim God's truth, they challenge the pseudo-reality that surrounds us. And so, God's enemies—Sin and Death—will work in our hearts and in our Christian communities to try make us ignore or underestimate the truth and power that these words unveil and unleash.

The challenge for us personally and communally is, through the power of God's Spirit, to discipline our hearts and minds to stay open to the gospel, for it is God's power and in it the righteousness of God is revealed from faith for faith. As it is written, the one who is righteous by faith shall live.

Scripture: Romans 1:16–17

Questions:

1. What are some of the different ways "the righteousness of God" has been understood?

2. What connections might we see between faith and righteousness, between faith and justice?

3. How might we hear Paul's words with fresh ears and attentive hearts so that "the righteousness of God" leads us into life?

6

He Even Milks the Cows
through You

Stephen Andrews

> "And to the man he said: 'cursed is the ground
> because of you: in toil you shall eat of it all the
> days of your life'" (Gen 3:17b).

In his humorous travel guide to boating on the Thames,
the Victorian author Jerome K. Jerome remarks, "I like
work; it fascinates me. I can sit and look at it for hours."[1]
Jerome's quip is funny because it trades on a common
irony about work and the way that work is perceived by
the "leisured class." The irony is that work is essential to an
economy that venerates leisure. In other words, for most
people in modern Western culture, we work not just to eat,
but to make it possible *not* to work. We regard Wednesdays
as "hump days," and at the end of the week we say "TGIF."
We accumulate our hours so that we can enjoy time away
from work's sameness, stress, and soreness. And we hope
to have enough spare cash at the end of it all to pay for

---

1. Jerome, *Three Men in a Boat*, 144.

others to work, so that we too can be fascinated and "look at it for hours."

Why this antipathy towards work? Well, modern attitudes about work are complicated. It is true that they are affected by the seemingly universal aversion identified by Jerome. But in part they are also shaped by the capitalistic values that govern our society. Work is the means by which someone "earns a living" and pays his or her dues as a productive member of the body politic. In this respect, work has become a measure of utility, and it affects the way we view one another, and the way we view ourselves. Consequently, despite our allergy to work, we can feel guilty or anxious when we aren't working.

An article entitled "The 'Busy' Trap," written by Tim Kreider in the *New York Times* five years ago, captures this well. Commenting on the plague of frenzy that seems to characterize our generation, he opines:

> It's become the default response when you ask anyone how they're doing: "Busy!" "*So* busy." "*Crazy* busy." It is, pretty obviously, a boast disguised as a complaint. And the stock response is a kind of congratulation: "That's a good problem to have," or "Better than the opposite."[2]

But he continues: "Busyness serves as a kind of existential reassurance, a hedge against emptiness; obviously your life cannot possibly be silly or trivial or meaningless if you are so busy, completely booked, in demand every hour of the day." And who does Kreider say is ultimately responsible for this modern addiction to busyness? "The Puritans turned work into a virtue," he explains, "evidently forgetting that God invented it as a punishment." His solution, of

2. Kreider, "The 'Busy' Trap," https://opinionator.blogs.nytimes.com/2012/06/30/the-busy-trap/.

course, is to be found in promoting what he describes as "defiant indolence" and "resolute idleness."[3]

The idea that work comes to us as a drudgery does have some resonance in Scripture, as we learn in Genesis 3. Furthermore, I believe it is true that Protestant thought on the nature of vocation and predestination has helped to shape perceptions of work that are fundamentally unhealthy, that make "crazy busy" truly crazy. But in a series of essays where we are thinking with the reformers about key biblical texts, I want to take time to draw out some of the reformers' insights as a way of helping us to discover a more wholesome view of work. Briefly, I want to elaborate on three Reformed ideas: a) that human beings were made for work, b) that human toil can be a means of grace, and c) that the preeminent aim of work is the love of God and neighbor.

So, to begin with, human beings were made for work. The reformers remind us that Genesis 3:17–19 is not the first biblical reference to work. Immediately after the creation of the human being in Genesis 2:7, we are told that "The Lord God planted a garden in Eden away to the east, and in it he put the man he had formed." God then carries on the work of a landscaper, adding trees and rivers, precious metals and stones. And then, in 2:15, we read that "The Lord God took the man and put him in the Garden of Eden to till it and look after it." Luther comments here that "it is appropriate to point out that man was created not for leisure but for work, even in the state of innocence."[4]

Mesopotamian epics had their own accounts of how the human workforce came to be. But there people were created to be slaves to the gods, waiting on their needs and

3. Ibid.

4. Luther, *Lectures on Genesis*, 103.

attending to menial tasks that were tiresome to them. In contrast, the biblical account furnishes an image of human beings cooperating with God in the management of the garden he had called Eden, "delight." There is, of course, a parallel here with God's earlier commission to humanity, where he also shared with them the dominion of the earth (Gen 1:28).

So from the beginning human beings are meant to find fulfilment in work. Dorothy Sayers said, "Work is not primarily a thing one does to live, but the thing one lives to do."[5] This is not to deny that the joy of co-laboring with God in the world is frequently elusive. But it is right that we should receive a sense of satisfaction in our work and experience pride in a job well done. For there is a dignity in labor that is a consequence of our having been created in the image of him whose care for us and for creation is ongoing. In the words of the Psalmist: "He sendeth the springs into the valleys / they run among the hills. [. . .] He watereth the hills from above; / the earth is filled with the fruit of his works" (Ps 104:10, 13).[6]

But then, secondly, human toil can be a means of grace. It is well that we seek gratification in our labor, and that we strive to provide humane and profitable conditions for those who work for and alongside us. But the hard reality of our existence is that we no longer live in God's garden of delight. Where we may hope to receive some degree of enjoyment from our work, in the end, we sometimes need to work simply to survive. And even with survival as a motive, we may come to regard our employment as a place of overwhelming frustration and futility.

5. Sayers, *Creed or Chaos*, 53.
6. *Book of Common Prayer*, 462–63.

Now we have come to the world of Genesis 3. Here Luther says, "work, which in the state of innocence would have been play and joy, is a punishment."[7] Indeed, for Luther, the punishment is more severe for us than for Adam because of the growth of sin in the world. But the infestation of thorns and thistles provides us this service: they stir us in our insensibility and awaken memories of our waywardness and its consequences. Comments Luther,

> Not only in the churches, therefore, do we hear ourselves charged with sin. All the fields, yes, almost the entire creation is full of such sermons, reminding us of our sin and of God's wrath, which has been aroused by our sin.[8]

In this Luther would seem to be following Chrysostom, who held that the condemnation to a life of toil and labor is so "you may never forget your disobedience."[9]

Remembering our disobedience is never a pleasant occupation in itself. Indeed, it can be humiliating, quite literally as we grovel in the dust. And yet it can be a means of grace if it leads to repentance and trust. Luther, like Cranmer after him, understood the dynamics of the human soul. The contrition that God plants in our hearts when we remember our sin leads to a sure confidence in Jesus Christ as the sin-bearer. The fruitlessness of the earth should make us think of "the promise of the Seed," says Luther, "who will remove the penalty of eternal death, which is infinitely greater." For Tertullian, the very symbols of our sins in the thorns and thistles are now borne by the Savior as a spiny crown.

7. Luther, *Lectures on Genesis*, 102–3.

8. Ibid., 209.

9. Chrysostom, "Baptismal Instructions," 2.4.5.

And this leads, finally, to the conviction that the pre-eminent aim of work is the love of God and neighbor. Martin Luther's greatest contribution to Christian thought in this area had to do with his view of "vocation." He rejected the notion that "vocation" was restricted to those under vows in the church or monastery. He and Calvin taught that, as the first man received a commission as a farmer, the divine call is issued to all human beings to join him in his work in the world, and therefore all of life and its godly activities are sanctified. This means that all mundane enterprises, domestic, economic, political, educational, and cultural, are infused with a religious significance. False is the separation of the sacred and the profane, as well as the social pyramid that holds bishops in higher esteem than bakers. True is the reality that God and his human creation are meant to work in partnership with him and with one another.

And it is with this thought that we will end. Luther held that all work, when done in the right spirit and trusting in God, embodies the Christian vocation. Therefore, when we serve others, we participate with God in forwarding his purposes for humanity. And when we are served by another, we are being served by the God who has called them to their task. In Luther's famous expression, "God milks the cows through the hands of the milkmaid." When we pray to God to "give us this day our daily bread," we must be prepared to see his answer in the farmer that grows the grain and harvests the crop, in the miller who grinds the corn, in the baker who cooks the bread, in the driver who transports the bread to market, and in the shopkeeper who sells the loaf to us. In this way we may understand all vocation, as Luther did, as the *larva dei*, the "mask of God," and we honor God when we detect him behind all honest work.[10]

So we work because we were made to work and because we can find fulfilment in it; we work to remind ourselves of our need for God and of one another; and we work to meet one another's needs and to glorify God. May our work, in this fallen world, be so used by him that we may see its completion in the vision of Isaiah, where the Lord says: "They shall build houses and inhabit them; they shall plant vineyards and eat their fruit. They shall not build and another inhabit; they shall not plant and another eat; for like the days of a tree shall the days of my people be, and my chosen shall long enjoy the work of their hands. They shall not labor in vain, or bear children for calamity; for they shall be offspring blessed by the Lord and their descendants as well" (Isa 65:21–23).

Scripture: Genesis 3:17–19

Questions

1. What are some of the reasons we often find it confusing to understand the significance of work in the context of the Christian life?

2. How might an understanding of toil as a means of grace help change our attitude towards work?

3. What might help us cultivate the understanding that our labor is an opportunity to join in God's work in the world?

10. See Wingren, *Luther on Vocation*, 9, 138.

7

On the Mountain with Jesus

Robert Dean

IN THE DRAMATIC CONCLUSION to the Gospel of Matthew, we are confronted by *Jesus on the Mountain*, the *Theologian of Christian Witness*, speaking of *The End of the Church*. Following *The Death of Jesus in Matthew*, this resurrection account stands *At the Heart of the Gospel*, allowing us to glimpse *Zion's Final Destiny*.[1] This passage has been described as the interpretive key to the Gospel of Matthew. As such, it should not surprise us to find that much of the Christian life and work is summed up in its verses.

This passage was also a favorite of the Protestant reformers, who frequently employed it for polemical purposes in their ongoing struggle with the Church of Rome. For example, Luther offers the following comments on Jesus' command to teach the nations to observe everything he has commanded: "See, here again [Jesus] does not say, 'Teach them to observe what you invent,' but 'what I have

---

1. The preceding sentences are largely composed of book titles (or parts of book titles) written by the following Wycliffe faculty members (in order of appearance): Terence Donaldson, Joseph Mangina, Ephraim Radner, Catherine Sider-Hamilton, Ann Jervis, and Christopher Seitz.

commanded you.' Therefore it cannot be otherwise: the pope and his bishops and teachers must be wolves and apostles of the devil, for they teach not the commands of Christ, but their own words."[2]

Ironically, the tendency for which Luther criticized the medieval church of his day has become the norm amongst all types of North American Christians in our day. According to the ground-breaking sociological work of Christian Smith and Melinda Lundquist Denton, the predominant operative theology in North American congregations today is a mutation of the Christian faith which they call "Moralistic Therapeutic Deism," or MTD for short.[3] The term "Moralistic Therapeutic Deism" reflects three of the main tenets of this theologically transmitted disease that has infected North American Christianity. It is moralistic because it believes that religion is about being good, nice, and fair to one another. It is therapeutic because it believes the primary goal of life is to be happy and to feel good about oneself. Finally, it is deistic because it believes in a vague god who does not need to be particularly involved in one's life, unless there is some sort of crisis to be resolved. In many ways, this is the perfect religion for a culture of consumers, as it allows people to pick and choose from the buffet of religious options on offer and fashion their own "choose your adventure" form of spirituality. Whereas Luther, when summoned to appear before the Imperial Diet at Worms, boldly declared, "my conscience is captive to the Word of God,"[4] today many of his Protestant descendants seem to be saying, "the Word of God is captive to my conscience."

2. Martin Luther, "Avoiding the Doctrines of Men," 148.

3. Smith and Denton, *Soul Searching*.

4. Luther, "Martin Luther at the Diet of Worms," 112.

We have made ourselves the measure of all things. We modern people call this freedom. The Bible describes this condition as the slavery of sin. Martin Luther could speak of the human being under the power of sin as existing in a state of what he called *cor curvum in se*—"the heart turned in upon itself." For Luther, the fallen human being suffers from a form of radical egocentricity in which the heart is like a black hole which threatens to draw everything into its crushing gravitational field. The Scottish writer and pastor George MacDonald incisively cut to the heart of this matter when he wrote, "the one principle of hell is—I am my own. I am my own king and my own subject."[5]

Luther knew that to be saved is to be liberated from the reign of our sovereign selves and set free to love the Lord our God with all our heart and with all our soul and with all our mind and with all our strength and to love our neighbor as ourselves. This freedom comes through the proclamation of the gospel received in faith. But the gospel, for Luther, is nothing other than the story of a king. "The gospel," Luther writes, "is a story about Christ, God's and David's Son, who died and was raised and is established as Lord. This is the gospel in a nutshell."[6] Christ has redeemed us from the power of sin, death, and the devil, Luther elsewhere asserted, in order that "[we] may be his, live under him in his kingdom, and serve him in everlasting righteousness, innocence, and blessedness, even as he is risen from the dead and lives and reigns to all eternity."[7]

The good news of the gospel is the story of a king—the true King. Our passage from Matthew 28 depicts the enthronement of that king on his holy mountain. Earlier

5. MacDonald, *Unspoken Sermons*, 332.

6. Luther, "A Brief Instruction," 118.

7. Luther, "The Small Catechism," 480.

on another high mountain, the devil had offered Jesus all the kingdoms of the world, but on that occasion Jesus sent Satan scurrying away, tail between his legs, by reciting God's Word. Now, on this mountain, we see that authority is entrusted not to a man who attempted to seize it through doing things his own way, but to the Son of Man who freely submitted to the will of his Father, enduring the shame of the cross. Here on the mountain, the Suffering Servant is revealed to be the Messiah of Israel. In this way, our reading from the Gospel of Matthew turns out to be an excellent prescription for combatting MTD. It simply needs to be topically applied.

Here on the mountain, we see that the Christian faith is not about being nice or good, it's about becoming holy. We have been enlisted by the King in the royal company of the saints. Terry Donaldson puts it like this: "In this command to make disciples who adhere to Jesus' teachings and who are visibly identified with him in baptism, we have the charter of the church, the constitution of the eschatological people of God."[8] The peculiar politics of this "Christian holy people" is embodied in distinct practices like the preaching of the Word, the celebration of baptism and Eucharist, the exercise of the keys, appointing people to offices within the church, prayer, public praise, and thanksgiving, and discipleship under the sign of the cross. Luther tells us these are the ordinary means through which "the Holy Spirit not only sanctifies his people, but also blesses them."[9]

Here on the mountain, we see that the Christian faith is not about choosing our own adventure, it's about being caught up in "an adventure we didn't know we wanted to

8. Donaldson, *Jesus on the Mountain*, 182.

9. Luther, "On the Councils and the Church," 165–66.

be on."[10] We have been given a purpose beyond anything our fleeting and confused personal desires could ever provide   we have been made ambassadors of the King. Our royal commission is to go into all the world proclaiming the reign of the Lord of Life and bearing witness to the presence of his peaceable kingdom as we enact our ministry of reconciliation. The long awaited eschatological pilgrimage of the nations to Zion for instruction in the ways of the Lord has begun in the sending forth of the disciples from the mountain to gather the nations under Christ's royal rule.

Here on the mountain, we see that the Christian faith is not about a god who stays at a distance, it's about the Lord who draws near. When the disciples saw the risen Jesus, they worshipped him—a most peculiar thing for good Jews to do, for there is only One worthy of worship. Yet, as the encounter unfolds, we are given an indication that the disciples' inkling was correct. Matthew ends with Jesus' promise, "I am with you always to the end of the age," which brings us back full circle to the beginning of Matthew, where the child in Mary's womb is described as Emmanuel—"God with us." Our God does not remain safely shut up within a realm of celestial security, but comes to us in flesh and bone and alights upon us in gentle breath and gusting wind. It is fitting that this passage would introduce the baptismal formula, for both our holy identity and divine vocation flow from our immersion in the love that has been shared from all eternity between the Father and the Son in the Holy Spirit.

In this we find ourselves not merely standing *before* the dramatic conclusion to Matthew's Gospel, we find ourselves standing *within* it. The pilgrimage of the nations to

10. Hauerwas, "Christianity," 531.

Zion has begun, and we Gentiles "who once were far off have been brought near by the blood of Christ" (Eph 2:13) and are made to be members of God's royal family—*sola gratia*! We have been grafted into Messiah's people and given a new way of life in which we are learning to obey all that our Master has commanded us—*sola Scriptura*! The Lord has promised to be with us always, to the end of the age. By faith we cling to this unfailing Word—*sola fide*! Christ the King has triumphed over sin, death and the devil and has been entrusted with all authority in heaven and on earth—*solus Christus*! We are God's people, immersed by the Holy Spirit in the depths of the Father's undying love for His Son, so that the Lord's reign of life may be made manifest to the nations as God's love overflows through us—*soli Deo gloria*!

Scripture: Matthew 28:16–20

Questions

1. What do you think might be some of the symptoms of "Moral Therapeutic Deism"? How might the spread of this theologically transmitted disease be combatted?

2. Read Isaiah 2:1–6, Ezekiel 34:25–31, and Daniel 7:13–14. How do these Old Testament passages enrich our understanding of Matthew 28:16–20?

3. Matthew 28:19 is often popularly referred to as the "Great Commission." Has the author's attempt to situate this verse within its immediate context in the book of Matthew, its larger context within the canon as a whole, and in light of the Christian theological

tradition challenged or enlarged your understanding
of the "Great Commission"? If so, how?

8

Come Back to Me
with All Your Heart

Catherine Sider-Hamilton

"You shall love the Lord your God with all your
heart and with all your soul and with all your
mind and with all your strength. This is the first
and great commandment and the second is like
it: you shall love your neighbor as yourself."

How is this possible?

For God is a hidden God—*deus absconditus*—and
the more we seek to look upon his face, the more we seek
to see his glory in the things he has made, the more we
strive to rise toward him by the works of our hands and the
strength of our mind, the farther we are from the knowledge and love of God. This is for Luther the anguish of the
human being, *Anfechtung*, and it is an anguish not only of
the mind but of the hands and heart.[1] For we are called to
love the holy and righteous One, to live holy and righteous

1. For an excellent and approachable discussion of *Anfechtung*
in the context of Luther's theology of the cross, see McGrath, *Luther's
Theology of the Cross*, 201–28.

as the One we love, to live in love for each other, and it is not what we do.

William Cavanaugh, in *Being Consumed*, tells the story of a mother and her daughter. The mother works in a factory in El Salvador making jackets for the Liz Claiborne clothing line. "The jackets sell for $178 each in the United States; the workers who make them earn 77 cents per jacket, or 56 cents an hour."[2] On these wages the mother is unable to feed herself and her daughter, who is three years old; her daughter drinks coffee because they cannot afford milk. "You shall love your neighbor as yourself." "I do not understand my own actions," Paul says. "For I do not do what I want, but what I hate—this I do" (Rom 7:15).

There is an anguish at the heart of things. About this, Luther was right. It is an anguish that stems from the distance of our hearts from God. Every one of us, if we are honest, knows this anguish. But it is not only personal. It is systemic.

The world, Luther says, is bent on power or riches or happiness or pleasure or a life of ease. So it was in the days of the old pagans. "[E]veryone made his god that which his heart was inclined [toward]."[3] So it is with us. Cavanaugh sets the story of the mother and her daughter who make our clothes while they faint with hunger in the context of the free market. They are paid what they are paid because that is what the market will bear. The market, the noted economist Milton Friedman says with approval, "gives people what they want." It gives people what they want "instead of what a particular group thinks they ought to

2. Cavanaugh, *Being Consumed*, 16.

3. From Luther's "Large Catechism," cited in Kilcrease and Lutzer, *Martin Luther in His Own Words*, 164.

want."[4] It is, precisely, free. Free for what? Free for whatever we want. It is, Friedman notes, the first and great commandment of the capitalist economy—that everyone should be free to seek their own desires without hindrance from anyone else. It is how the system works. *Free at last*! Here we are in the world we have made, free at last. Individual desire untrammeled, without God or common end. Our lives turned inward, to the devices and desires of our own hearts.

In this world defined by desire and the individual we are good at diversity. Consider the recent pastoral statement of the Anglican Diocese of Toronto: *A Pastoral Commitment to Diverse Theological Positions.* Freedom to believe, with respect to marriage and sex in particular, whatever I want, to seek whatever I want, to live in the way I choose. The individual and my desire at the heart of all things. The church *not* as communion, but as an association of sovereign individuals. This is the culture of capitalism. It is the free market take-over of the church.

But where in this is the heart that clings to God? That "cling[s] to him with the heart," as Luther says, so that "the heart knows no other comfort or confidence than in him and does not suffer to be torn from him but, for him, risks and disregards everything on earth."[5] *Everything* on earth. The heart that is not its own, that by some miracle of grace longs not for its own devices and desires but for God? The heart that Augustine discovered and announces with joy on the very first page of his *Confessions*: "You have made us for yourself, O God, and our hearts are restless until they find their rest in you." The heart that is not free, that is en-

4. Friedman, *Capitalism and Freedom*, 15. Cited in Cavanaugh, *Being Consumed*, 4.

5. "Large Catechism: The First Commandment," in Kilcrease and Lutzer, *Martin Luther in His Own Words*, 163.

thralled by God. *Paulos doulos Christou Iēsou,* Paul says at the beginning of Romans (Rom 1:1). Paul the slave of Jesus the Christ. Jesus is the Christ. And Paul is his slave. That is who he is. Paul does not—cannot—stand alone, and this is his joy and his song. Paul's good news is that he is not free, he is not sovereign, even and especially over his own heart and soul and mind and desire. He is bound always and forever to Jesus, who loved him and gave himself for him. "For to me to live is Christ," Paul says, "and to die is gain" (Phil 1:21).

Diversity, this free market of the sovereign individual, is pretty thin stuff. It offers us tolerance, individuals getting along together for the satisfaction of each individual's wants.

Jesus, though . . . Jesus offers us love. "A new commandment I give to you. Love one another as I have loved you" (John 13:34, 15:12). See what a love it is, this love of the Lord. For Jesus comes to us here where we are, slaves to our own desires, turned by our own will and beyond the power of our own will in upon ourselves, forsaking each other in the desires of our hearts, in the desires of our hearts God-forsaking. Here Jesus comes to us, here he stands in our midst and reaches out his hands in love to us, and when we do not come to him, when we turn upon him and upon each other instead, he gives himself for us.

"It is necessary for the Son of Man to suffer many things and to be rejected by the elders and chief priests and scribes and to be killed and after three days to rise" (Mark 8:31). Three times Jesus has said it, this passion prediction, before the scribe asks his question in Mark's gospel. It is necessary for the Son of Man to suffer and die. Why is it necessary? Because we turn away, from Eden to this day, and when God turns to us in love, in the Child of his own heart, we do not turn to him. Jesus Christ crucified is the God-forsakenness of our hearts.

Jesus Christ crucified is our God-forsakenness lifted up in his outstretched arms into the love of God. Christ died for us. While we were yet sinners, Christ died for us. Paul cannot get over it. *Eti gar Christos*—still, while we were still sinners, Christ! Christ died for us! God is not God of the dead but of the living. We are quite wrong, in the *telos*-free market of our hearts. There is a resurrection. There is a heart that may be turned to God again. There is a new life. "I have been crucified with Christ," Paul says. "I live no longer. The life I now live in the flesh I live in faith in the Son of God. I live no longer, but Christ lives in me. Christ, who loved me and gave himself for me" (Gal 2:19, 20). It was, Professor David Demson has said, perhaps Luther's favorite verse. It is our hope.

"St. Paul preaches the true liturgy," Luther says, "and makes all his Christians priests, so that they may offer not money or cattle as priests do in the law, but their own bodies, putting their desires to death."[6] My body an offering to God by the grace of God in Christ, my life no longer my own but his, and in him my neighbor's. My life an offering to God and to my neighbor from a heart seized and pierced and radiant, a heart enthralled by the love of God in Jesus Christ our Lord.

"Come back to Me . . . with all your heart. For you are precious in My sight, and honored, and I love you" (Deut 30:2, Isa 43:4).

Scripture: Mark 12:20–31

6. "Preface to St. Paul's Letter to the Romans," in Kilcrease and Lutzer, *Martin Luther in His Own Words*, 67.

Questions

1. What are some of the "gods" or idols who capture our hearts, misshape our desires, and shape the world around us?

2. How do we live with the tension (or anguish) of the call to love God with all our hearts and the reality that we seek fulfillment in many things other than God?

3. What are some practical ways we together can learn to live repentance—regularly returning to God with all our hearts?

9

The Reformation Principle We Might Want to Forget

The Pope as Antichrist

Alan Hayes

From its origins, Wycliffe College has identified itself with the theology of the English Reformation, which we summarize in what we now call the Six Principles. These include the supremacy of Scripture, justification by grace through faith alone, the church as the blessed company of all faithful people, the sufficiency of Christ's sacrifice, the priesthood of all believers, and the presence of Christ in the hearts of those who faithfully receive Holy Communion. But there's one principle that's missing from this list, a principle that was repeated again and again by the reformers, a principle which for some of them was the most important one of all. That's the principle that *the pope is antichrist*.

To be clear, I'm personally very happy that this principle was *not* included in the Six Principles of Wycliffe

College. For me, it's one of the embarrassments of the Reformation. At the time of the Reformation it was an essential justification for schism, but as such it was an assertion of self-righteousness by reformers whose own hands were not always clean. The reformers often overlooked Paul's injunction in his letter to the Philippians, "In humility regard others as better than yourselves." So why do we include this principle among the topics of this book? The reason is that, in a book on the teachings of the Reformation, honesty compels us to acknowledge this one. Most of my fellow writers here have congratulated the Reformation on rediscovering deep truths of the gospel; but here is another side to the Reformation, a darker side, which we need to face as well.

For the 500th anniversary of the Reformation, our Toronto School of Theology community, like many communities around the world, came together for a service of worship that had been designed by Roman Catholics and Lutherans. In that service, we recognized together blessings in the Reformation for which to praise God, and we acknowledged errors and expressions of human pride to lament and confess. The historical fact is that the Reformation devolved into two main opposing sides that could not hear each other, that condemned each other, and that ultimately went to war against each other. It was not just that the reformers said to their adversaries, "We're right and you're wrong," which would have been bad enough. They went further and said, "*We* are on God's side, but *you* are ruled by the antichrist," and then they used Scripture as a weapon.

Pretty much all the reformers affirmed that the pope is the antichrist—except for the ones who said that the office of the papacy was antichrist, not just any one individual pope; and except for the ones who said that the pope and his minions were antichrists in the plural, or a collective antichrist; and except for the gentler reformers who said more modestly that the antichrist works through the office of the papacy. But despite the variations, the main theme was this: if you want to find the antichrist, go to the Vatican. Martin Luther was convinced that the pope was antichrist by 1520. That affirmation is in the Smalcald Articles, the doctrinal confessional statement of the Lutheran territories that banded together in 1531; and the Smalcald articles were put into the main confessional statement of Lutheranism, the Book of Concord.[1] The pope as antichrist gets a whole chapter in Calvin's *Institutes*.[2] The last words of a 67-year-old Thomas Cranmer, archbishop of Canterbury and the main author of our Book of Common Prayer, as he was being burned at the stake on the instructions of a Roman Catholic queen of England, were: "As for the pope, I refuse him, as Christ's enemy, and antichrist, with all his false doctrine."[3] For centuries, Anglicans knew that whatever else we were, we weren't papists. That was a cornerstone of our identity. Other Protestant churches thought the same. To me, growing up in the years before Vatican II, the gulf between Roman Catholics and Protestants felt about as wide as the Atlantic Ocean. My parents were happy for me to go after school into the homes of my Jewish friends or into the homes of friends who were members of visible minorities, but once when I invited a Roman Catholic playmate to a birthday party, they clearly expressed their discomfort.

1. "Smalcald Articles," II.ii.25, II.iv.10, II.iv.12, III.xi.1.

2. *Institutes of the Christian Religion*, IV.7.

3. Foxe, *Unabridged Acts and Monuments Online*, 11:2015. http://www.johnfoxe.org.

About a dozen passages were used by the reformers to think about the antichrist. Not many of these passages use the actual term "antichrist," which appears only in the first two letters of John. There it is used usually in the singular but also in the plural to refer to one who will come when the end is near and will deny that Jesus is the word of God, and will embody opposition to Jesus (1 John 2:18, 22; 4:3; 2 John 7). Other passages in the Bible speak to the idea of antichrist. In Daniel 7, which describes Daniel's vision of four beasts coming out of the sea, the fourth is a terrifying beast, part human and part animal, with ten horns, who makes war on the saints until he is conquered. The reformers identified that as a prophecy of the antichrist. In 2 Thessalonians 2, Paul does not use the term antichrist, but talks about the man of lawlessness who will take his seat in the temple of God and then declare that he himself is God. This too has appeared to commentators as a reference to the antichrist. The idea of the antichrist has also been found in some apocalyptic passages in the synoptic gospels that speak of a false messiah, as well as in passages in Isaiah, Ezekiel, and Revelation (Matt 24:27–31; Mark 13:6; Luke 21:25–28; Isa 14:13–14; Ezek 28:2ff.; Rev 13).

Because the antichrist was to come at the end of human history, it was often part of passionate speculation about what will happen before Christ comes again, and of course those discussions are continuing in many places today. Some of the reformers were very interested in that kind of millennial expectation, while others were not. Just so as not to get too complicated, for present purposes I will leave the millennialist dimension of this topic to one side.

Now, even before the Reformation, there was a centuries-long history of people saying that the pope was antichrist. The more the papacy asserted its authority both over the church and over the kingdoms of the world, the more doubts developed as to whether the papacy was really a holy thing. By about 1200, Pope Innocent III was declaring that those who were disobedient to the pope were outside the church and therefore could not be saved.[4] It looked to some as if he was claiming God's authority, reminiscent of Paul's warning to the Thessalonians that a lawless man claiming to be God would take up residence in the temple of God. And the optics got even worse during the Renaissance, when a series of ultra-worldly, more or less debauched popes came along. It looked to many as if a person who represented the opposite of Christian morality and doctrine was pre-empting Christ himself.

Probably the most influential medieval writer along these lines was John Wyclif, an Oxford don in the fourteenth century. He was writing during the great western schism, when there were two rival popes, one in Rome and one in Avignon in what's now southern France; different countries in their different alliances supported different popes, which made the papacy look totally worldly and political. And Wyclif came up with twelve antitheses to show that the pope was the opposite of Christ, and therefore the antichrist.[5] Here are a few of them:

- Christ is the truth: the pope teaches falsehood.

- Christ embraces poverty: the pope embraces wealth.

- Christ values gentleness and humility: the pope sends out armed crusades.

---

4. Innocent III was the first pope who regularly styled himself "the vicar of Christ," reflecting his claim on the obedience of all Christians.

5. Buck, *The Roman Monster*, 82–83.

- Christ establishes the law of love: the pope promulgates laws that oppress the faithful.

- Christ sends missionaries into the world: the pope sanctions monasteries so that people can leave the world.

- Christ renounces secular power: the pope claims dominion over all kingdoms.

- Christ chose twelve humble disciples: the pope appoints rich worldly cardinals.

- Christ willingly suffers: the pope wages war.

- Christ serves others: the pope demands homage.

Wyclif's own conclusion from this was that the real church of Christ is not the prominent institution organized around a hierarchy extending down from the papacy; the real church of Christ is the company of the elect, and since we cannot know for sure until the last day who is among the company of the elect, the true church is invisible. In particular, Wyclif says, we have no way of knowing in this life that the pope is among the elect, so obeying him is a very risky thing to do.

We can agree, with Wyclif, that there is reason to be suspicious of the teaching, values, and actions of the leaders of the visible church. Of course, the logic of Wyclif's suspicion of the claims of the visible church extends to all visible churches, not just the Roman Catholic Church. The reformers recognized that all our churches sometimes go astray, even badly astray, and that they are continually needing to be reformed. We can also agree that Christian leaders who are lacking in Christian integrity in their faith and morals model something anti-Christ, not pro-Christ. The problem is that sometimes the reformers ignored their own logic and spoke as if the leaders who dishonor the gospel in their doctrine and morals exist only in other people's churches, not their own. The further problem is that we might draw the false conclusion that if we make a church for ourselves, we can avoid the sin and worldliness and faithlessness of other people's churches, and do things right. Schism starts out looking for reform and renewal; it winds up in self-righteousness and self-justification, and calling outsiders names. We can be so intent on finding the mote in our brother or sister's eye that we fail to consider the beam in our own eye. We can rightly criticize the wealth of the Renaissance papacy, but we had also better remember the much greater wealth that the Anglican Church of Canada has reaped from its interests in land that was seized from indigenous peoples, and our church's many excuses as to why it shouldn't make restitution.

Recently the Methodist theologian Stanley Hauerwas wrote a column in the *Washington Post* that shows how little the divisions of the Reformation apply today.[6] In fact, he confesses that he is frankly confused about what the Protestant Reformation even means, five hundred years later. The way he puts it is that Protestantism won; today, after the Second Vatican Council, the Roman Catholic Church clearly affirms the authority of Scripture, the centrality of Christ, and the importance of conducting worship in the language of the people, all among the chief points of the Protestant reformers. And it certainly no longer sells indulgences. So, Hauerwas asks, why are we not Catholic? What is the rationale for being Protestant, given that our Protestant churches themselves are not so spectacularly principled and holy? As he says, "Each Protestant church tries to be just different enough from other

6. Hauerwas, "The Reformation is Over."

Protestant churches to attract an increasingly diminishing market share." In fact, he goes on to say, the Roman Catholic Church has become quite attractive to committed Christians because it has an intellectually rich theological tradition that can negotiate the "acids of our culture." The best reason he can offer for remaining Protestant, aside from the fact that his wife is an ordained minister, is that the church needs faithful outsiders who have not been co-opted by the ecclesiastical status quo and are free to critique it when it falls short of God's mission for it. That may not be our answer, but the point is that it has long since ceased to be possible for us, if it ever was, to claim that the Roman Catholic Church is controlled by the antichrist, while Protestant churches are faithful to the pure Word of God.

So the scriptures about the antichrist are first of all a reality check telling us that the gospel of Christ has its enemies, and that some of those enemies have prestigious and influential seats in the temple of God. Secondly, they give us hope, assuring us that in the end the antichrist will be vanquished and God's sovereignty over all creation will be clearly seen. And if we look at the scriptures about the antichrist in the context of other scriptures that warn us against justifying ourselves, against judging others more harshly than ourselves, against deceiving ourselves that there is no sin in us, they invite us to be discerning about whom we decide to follow, and wise about whom we decide to accuse. For that warning, and for that hope, and for that invitation, thanks be to God.

Scripture: 2 Thessalonians 2:3 and Daniel 7:8

Questions

1. "Schism starts out looking for reform and renewal; it winds up in self-righteousness and self-justification, and calling outsiders names." What are some examples of how division often results in an inability to see our own prejudices?

2. How might a deeper understanding of the history of division in the church help us learn how to find a way forward together?

3. What does it mean to be faithful when we are in deep disagreement with the leadership in our own church or churches? What does it mean to be faithful when we perceive our church acting in ways that appear to contradict the gospel?

10

Real Worship

Thomas P. Power

"HERE MAY ALL MANNER of persons, men, women, young, old, learned, unlearned, rich, poor, priests, laymen, lords, ladies, officers, tenants, and mean men, virgins, wives, widows, lawyers, merchants, artificers, husbandmen, and all manner of persons of what estate or condition soever they be, may in this book learn all things what they ought to believe, what they ought to do, and what they should not do, as well concerning almighty God, as also concerning themselves and all other."[1]

These words, commending the study of Scripture, were written in 1540 by Thomas Cranmer, the chief architect of the English Reformation, in his famous preface to a revised translation of the Bible known as the Great Bible. In the same vein, Cranmer continued: "every man that cometh to the reading of this holy book, ought to bring with him first and foremost this fear of almighty God, and then next, a firm and stable purpose to reform his own self according thereunto, and so to continue,

1. Cranmer, "Preface to the Great Bible," http://www.bible-researcher.com/cranmer.html.

proceed, and prosper from time to time, showing himself to be a sober and fruitful hearer and learner."[2] If he does so, Cranmer maintains, that person will be able to teach by good example of life. However, the person who comes to Scripture otherwise—in Cranmer's words, "he that intermeddleth with this book," by which he meant, as he says elsewhere in his preface, with "superfluous contention and sophistication"[3]—will bring on himself the same consequences for the wicked as recorded in Psalm 50:16–23.

What did the words of these verses contain that were so serious that they represent God's reprimand to the wicked and act as a cautionary point of reference for Cranmer? To answer this question, we need to consider the psalm as a whole. The psalm is a liturgy or part of a liturgy associated with the renewal of the covenant by the people of Israel. The first part (Ps 50:1–15) sees God summoning his people because, though they know what to do, they misunderstand the meaning of sacrifice. They perform the prescribed rituals and ceremonies of worship mechanically, and are good at external observance. But they don't recognize that God has no need of such sacrifices, and their motives are insincere. Their formalism in worship is condemned. The solution, God commands them, is not to abandon ritual and sacrifice altogether, but to bring to it a real disposition of thanksgiving that animates it.

How to do this? God tells them: "Call upon me in the day of trouble, and I will deliver you, and you will honor me" (Ps 50:15). So all sacrifice is worthless unless it is in thanksgiving for the way God has heard our cries and petitions, how we acknowledge his provision, and how we respond with praise. God is to be worshipped in reverence

2. Ibid.

3. Ibid.

and awe, not with empty formalism. As the verse in the more well-known psalm that follows this one says: "The sacrifices of God are a broken spirit; a broken and contrite heart, O God, you will not despise" (Ps 51:17).

The Wicked

God then switches his attention to a second group—the wicked (Ps 50:16–21). Who were the wicked and what made them so? They were not pagans or non-believers. They were those who knew and could recite the law but did not keep it in practice. They accept God's word as true and right, but as Calvin says in his commentary on this psalm, when it comes "to regulate their conduct, and restrain their sinful affections, they dislike and detest it."[4] What benefit is it to be able to recite the law if they hate God's discipline, if they ignore God's word, and if their moral and ethical conduct is questionable? It makes their worship superficial and false. The main charge against them, therefore, is hypocrisy.

The charge of hypocrisy is illustrated specifically in relation to their breaking of three of the commandments. The eighth commandment says: "You shall not steal." But they "see a thief" and "join with him" (Ps 50:18a), in other words cooperating as friends with thieves. Here is dishonesty. The seventh commandment says: "You shall not commit adultery." But they "throw in your lot with adulterers" (Ps 50:18b), in other words keeping company with adulterers. Here is disloyalty. The ninth commandment says: "You shall not bear false witness against your neighbor." But the wicked "use your mouth for evil and harness your tongue

4. Calvin, "Psalm 50," http://www.sacred-texts.com/chr/calvin/cc09/cc09015.htm.

to deceit. You speak continually against your brother and slander your own mother's son" (Ps 50:19–20). In other words, they do not control what they say and they speak badly of family members.

What makes matters worse is that they assume from God's silence that they will not be called to account, and that such silence in their minds equates their behavior with God's. "Those things you have done and I kept silent; you thought I was altogether like you" (Ps 50:21).

How can such people enter into God's presence in worship and recite his laws? They can't. This way of living denies them the right to worship. In Calvin's words: "the ungodly . . . only aggravate their guilt by assuming the semblance of piety." Or as he says further, they are "those whose religion lies in an observance of ceremonies, with which they attempt to blind the eyes of God," and they display "the vanity of seeking to shelter impurity of heart and life under a veil of outward services."[5] The message is that faith and morality can't be separated as if the one is God's realm, and the moral order something different.

Those who speak of God's laws but don't keep them are similarly denounced by Jesus. In Matthew he is recorded as saying: "Woe to you teachers of the law and Pharisees, you hypocrites. You give a tenth of your spices: mint, dill, and cummin. But you have neglected the more important matters of the law: justice, mercy and faithfulness. You should have practiced the latter, without neglecting the former" (Matt 23:23). Here Jesus condemns the hypocrites who claimed to teach the law but in fact led their hearers astray because they did not practice it fully. The lesson for this second group is to know that God wants our moral life to coincide with our religious practice.

5. Ibid.

Conclusion

There are two groups identified in this psalm. One group knows what to do, the other knows what to say. Both are going through the motions of religious observance, playing at being religious. Neither know God at a deep level. So in this psalm God demands that his people recognize who he really is and what he expects of them.

Both groups are given a choice between their own destruction or their salvation. This salvation is held out to them as a promise: "He who sacrifices thank offerings honors me, and he prepares the way so that I may show him the salvation of God" (Ps 50:23). Salvation is available to those who attend to God's instruction, God's Word, God's way, and the obedience it demands in thought, word, and deed.

In some ways, what we might term "mechanical Christianity" was a general concern of the reformers and of Christian humanists like Erasmus. Thus practices such as indulgences, veneration of saints, and pilgrimages were expressive of an attempt to achieve salvation by artificial means and through merit. While humanists and reformers might agree on the nature of the problem, they disagreed profoundly on the solution to it. For Erasmus the solution lay in moral reform, whereas for Luther such a change would be transitory unless it was grounded in the doctrine that derived from the scriptural precept "the just shall live by faith" (Rom 1:17), which was the only corrective to a mechanical Christianity.

Yet despite the strictures of Scripture and the cautions of reformers like Cranmer and Calvin, all too easily do we measure our faith by the fulfillment of externals, religious busyness, keeping up appearances, and acting out of a sense of duty. Our tendency is to be contented with the performance of outward acts. We need to be concerned if our worship and prayer life are becoming formalities. And this psalm is a warning against formalism in what we say and do.

Remember what Moses did when he heard the following words from God: "The Lord, the Lord, the compassionate and gracious God, slow to anger, abounding in love and faithfulness, maintaining love to thousands, and forgiving wickedness, rebellion, and sin" (Exod 34:6). We are told that he "bowed to the ground at once and worshiped" (Exod 34:8). That is the disposition of heart and mind that we need to bring to our worship.

We need to examine our motives and realize that what God really wants is faithfulness to his Word, and evidence of our willingness to discern what that Word is telling us to do. Similarly our worship should not be focused on the externals, but on our personal response or dedication to the Lord, and must be based on a commitment to trust and obey Him.

Because God is intimately involved in the details of our lives, the lesson for us is to think of the whole array of involvements we have every day and ask ourselves the question: does our behavior or practice match our beliefs, faith, and commitments? Is there a disconnect between what we believe and what we do? The Ten Commandments are given to us as the discipline of moral living. For starters, consider the three mentioned here: honesty, loyalty, and slander? In these and in all manner of others, let it not be said of us, in Cranmer's words, that we were "idle babblers and talkers of the scripture out of season and all good order, without any increase of virtue, or example of good living."[6]

6. Cranmer, "Preface to the Great Bible."

Scripture: Psalm 50:16–23

Questions

1. What can we learn from this psalm about how to worship God?

2. How can we do our duty and fulfill our religious responsibilities without becoming simply formal or mechanical?

3. How do we give due attention to duty and at the same time not neglect works of "justice, mercy, and faithfulness"?

Power to the Priesthood
(of All Believers)

DAVID KUPP

THE PRIESTHOOD OF ALL believers is axiomatic for all Protestant ecclesiologies, thanks to Luther, Calvin, and the radical Protestants. As the waves of Reformation tumult and its counter-forces surged across Europe in the sixteenth century, the ripples generated by this doctrine of the priesthood of all believers rocked boats across the entirety of Christendom, from Rome to Constantinople to Armenia. Even though it was a central tenet within Protestantism, the priesthood of all believers became a deeply divisive issue of doctrine and practice.

I have three reflections to offer in this essay. First of all, I wonder if there is something both foundational and continuous about the priesthood of all believers, which links the ancient and the modern? Is there a First Principle behind the priesthood of all believers that reflects a social and religious organizing principle as old as humanity?

We employ First Principles regularly—in math, in science, in physics, and at least metaphorically in faith. For example, come with me for a moment to a warm autumn day some time ago in my back garden in Guelph. I was trying to remember how to solve for the hypotenuse. Do you recall that little formula? $A^2 + B^2 = C^2$. Otherwise known in the building trades as the "3-4-5 rule." If you have a right-angle triangle, and you add the square of side A plus the square of side B, the sum should equal the square of side C, the hypotenuse. We need to figure out these things, especially if it is Saturday afternoon, and you are trying to design Japanese ornamentation for the top of your new fence.

Many mathematical formulas are ancient, immutable First Principles at the heart of philosophy and logic. They have been applied for thousands of years to aesthetics, to the design of a chair, to the planning of a city, to the proportions of a chapel. Long before Pythagoras, Egyptian builders used ropes knotted in units of 3, 4, 5 to lay out perfect right angles. And the Babylonians also seem to have sorted out the secret of the hypotenuse centuries before the Greeks.

Perhaps even Jesus had experience of these mathematical First Principles? Think about it: in first-century Nazareth when a *tektón*—a carpenter—was hired to assemble and hang a door, the hypotenuse of the right-angle triangle would already have been familiar as a millennia-old mathematical principle that any apprentice must learn and practice for the trade.

Here's the point: I wonder if 1 Peter's "royal/holy priesthood" indicates a waypoint on a longer journey back to some First Principles of the human faith narrative, with stops along the way in Israel's liberation and prophetic texts. The implied egalitarian bent of 1 Peter's royal/holy priesthood may even ultimately be grounded in humanity's earliest hunter-gatherer and pastoralist era, when semi-mobile clans of indigenous peoples self-governed through relatively flat social structures. In Exodus 19:6 it was a re-forming group of landless, illiterate slaves who heard in their call to liberation: "you shall be to me a kingdom of priests and a holy nation." And again, later, in Israel's post-exilic restoration, "you shall be called priests of the Lord, you shall be named ministers of our God" (Isa 61:6). Centuries later, Jesus himself riles against the specialist religious castes, structures, and characters that had accrued excessive authority to themselves. They had lost this First Principle—the vision of becoming an entire "kingdom of priests"; they had ossified the Exodus liberation and the calls of Isaiah into rigid and exclusive socio-political religious institutions.

So our first reflection on the Reformation "priesthood of all believers" is how we might better comprehend its continuity in divine narrative history, even while seeing its flowering in the Reformation as a dramatic re-rendering of the ancient principle. If there is something about the priesthood of all believers that reflects a social and religious organizing principle as ancient as humanity, and as old as the Exodus call from slavery, then the Reformers were not only calling out Rome, but re-calling followers of Jesus to a social, political, economic, and religious life that echoes the gathered and liberated people of Yahweh.

So it was that Jesus' centripetal and centrifugal actions built a new form of community. Centripetal: he gathered the vulnerable, the marginalized, the children, the least ones to the center of this community. Centrifugal: he pushed the traditional socio-religious power brokers to the margins. There is much more to be explored here, but let's move on.

A second reflection: Even as there is something time-less and continuous about the priesthood of all believers, there's also something very new. Every context requires its re-adaptation, whether Exodus, Isaiah, first-century *ekkle-sia*, or Reformation.

- Martin Luther, the most prolific and important Protestant teacher on the priesthood of all believers, thought that "this word priest should become as com-mon as the word Christian" because all Christians are priests."[1] He touches on aspects of the doctrine in over fifty documents, and in fifteen of his writings he addresses it at length.[2] Luther identified preaching, sacrifice, and prayer as the central functions of the priesthood of all believers, but he also adds bearing the keys, judging doctrine, baptizing and celebrating the Eucharist.[3]

- Calvin's emphasis was more on the believer's priestly union with Christ and the resultant priestly access to the Father in prayer and Bible study. He also dis-cussed the priesthood of all believers in relation to vocations.

- A number of reformers and Anabaptists took stron-ger stances on a more radically egalitarian priest-hood, and at times they suffered dire consequences.

Five hundred years of Reformation evolution has delivered to us a wide continuum on the priesthood of all believers.

I grew up in a Baptist church that held strongly to its version of the priesthood of all believers. Over time I also

1. Luther, *Epistles of St. Peter and St. Jude*, 106. In Lindsley, "Priesthood of All Believers," 1 n.1.

2. Voss, *Priesthood of All Believers*, 259.

3. Ibid., 141.

sojourned within other Protestant communities that diversely held to this doctrine, among them the Anabaptists, Swedish Covenant, Methodists, and Anglicans. I realized over time that the priesthood of all believers is not a single doctrine but a broad continuum covering great diversity reflected in the schisms following Martin Luther and John Calvin.

What does this continuum look like? Imagine with me, if you will, on one end of the continuum an open-priesthood-of-all-believers—where all believers practice Luther's seven priestly functions. At the other end, only ordained priests can practice these functions. With these two poles setting the continuum, each person might determine for themselves where they or their community stand. Some might discover that even within one faith community the diverse understandings of the priesthood of all believers require more than a single position on the continuum. In other cases it might be instructive to reflect on how a church's official doctrine differs from its actual practice, and hence find that the two—doctrine and practice—occupy different positions along the continuum. The priesthood of all believers proves neither unanimous nor static.

A third reflection is that the reformers' and our own diversity on the priesthood of all believers drives us back into the heart of Scripture and its embedded call to reformation, to the "re-formation" of God's people. Engaging 1 Peter reminds us that the purpose of all ecclesiology is not to differentiate Baptist from Anglican, and Catholic from Orthodox. Ecclesiology is a diverse means to a common end, and our common end is to gather as the new community of Jesus, to worship and serve and be reunited with the Triune God, and to be reconciled with all of God's creation.

In 1 Peter 2 these reborn members of the community of Christ have their new identity established, and the shape of their new community is described in priesthood, temple, and sacrifice terms. Essentially, the formerly Jewish identity as God's people has now become theirs: they are now a priesthood to God. The building metaphor is rich with description. Community members are:

- Like a "spiritual house"—both as a new genre of household, built on Christ the living cornerstone, and in the process of becoming a holy temple of God.

- They are transformed into a holy priesthood, to offer spiritual sacrifices to God.

- In contrast with the stumbling rejecters, they receive four honorific titles (drawn from Exod 19:6 and Isa 43:20–21): But you are a chosen people, a royal priesthood, a holy people, God's own possession.

Christians in 1 Peter become identifiably God's own people.

> All the titles once attributed to Israel are ours. We are living stones of the spiritual temple, established on Jesus Christ as cornerstone, a holy priesthood offering spiritual sacrifices to God through our prayer, praise, worship, and daily living. The priesthood of the community is for the purpose of proclaiming God's mighty acts in Jesus, bringing us and others out of the darkness into the light.[4]

---

4. Watson and Callan, *First and Second Peter*, 52.

First Peter re-formed the gathered early church in the shape and function of Christ's spiritual house and holy priesthood, called to offer spiritual sacrifices. This the reformers understood to justify the priesthood of all believers. And they saw in it the teaching that any gathered member of that spiritual house and holy priesthood could lead their own spiritual fellowship. This of course came with risks and consequences, and much splintered diversity.

These brief explorations of the priesthood of all believers also uncover a lament among commentators: a lament that Reformation and Protestant ecclesiologies are in poor health. Voss refers to "the current ecclesial confusion" and calls for a fresh examination of the priesthood of all believers as a means of rejuvenation.[5] First Peter 2 is a good place to restart this critical re-formation dialogue. It completes

> the portrayal of the essence of Christian existence. Christian existence is lived out as the realization of community through koinonia and diakonia in the midst of society as one follows in discipleship the exalted Christ, who was rejected by society and now has become the foundation of a new form of shared, priestly gathering.[6]

"But you are a chosen race, a royal priesthood, a holy nation, God's own people, in order that you may proclaim the mighty acts of him who called you out of darkness into his marvelous light. Once you were not a people, but now you are God's people" (1 Pet 2:9, 10).

Scripture: 1 Peter 2:4–10

---

5. Voss, *Priesthood*, 2.

6. Goppelt, *A Commentary on 1 Peter*, 143.

Questions:

1. How does the understanding of the priesthood of all believers align with the words and images in the Gospels of Jesus forming and gathering his new community?

2. How did the reformers' various understandings of priesthood stand as a threat to the church in their era? How might these have exposed some of the abuses of clerical leadership?

3. If the current mixture of legacies in Western civilization (individualism, freedoms, democracy) has been decisively shaped by Protestant Christianity, what might the priesthood of all believers mean for emerging forms of democratic Christian gathering and ecclesiology? For the many calls for accountable and democratic governance across the world?

Bibliography

Barth, Karl. *The Epistle to the Romans*. Translated by Edwyn C. Hoskyns. 6th ed. London: Oxford University Press, 1995.

Book of Common Prayer (Canada). Toronto: Anglican Book Center, 1962.

Buck, Lawrence P. *The Roman Monster: An Icon of the Papal Antichrist in Reformation Polemics*. Early Modern Studies 13. Kirksville, MO: Truman State University Press, 2014.

Calvin, John. "Psalm 50." In *Psalms, Part II (Calvin's Commentaries 9)*, translated by John King. http://www.sacred-texts.com/chr/calvin/cc09/cc09015.htm.

Cavanaugh, William T. *Being Consumed: Economics and Christian Desire*. Grand Rapids, MI: Eerdmans, 2008.

Chrysostom, Saint John. "Baptismal Instructions." *Ancient Christian Writers* 31. Edited by Johannes Quasten and Walter J. Burghardt. Mahwah, NJ: Paulist, 1963.

Cranmer, Thomas. "Preface to the Great Bible." http://www.bible-researcher.com/cranmer.html.

Donaldson, Terence L. *Jesus on the Mountain: A Study in Matthean Theology*. Journal for the Study of the New Testament, Supplement Series 8. Sheffield: JSOT, 1985.

Foxe, John. *The Unabridged Acts and Monuments Online (TAMO)*. 1570 edition. HRI Online, Sheffield, 2011. http://www.johnfoxe.org.

Friedman, Milton. *Capitalism and Freedom*. Chicago, IL: University of Chicago Press, 1962.

Gaventa, B. Roberts. "The Cosmic Power of Sin in Paul's Letter to the Romans: Towards a Widescreen Edition." *Interpretation* (July 2004) 229–40.

Goppelt, Leonhard. *A Commentary on 1 Peter*. Grand Rapids: Eerdmans, 1993.

Hauerwas, Stanley. "Christianity: It's Not a Religion, It's an Adventure." In *The Hauerwas Reader*, edited by John Berkman and Michael Cartwright, 522–38. Durham: Duke University Press, 2001.

———. "The Reformation is over. Protestants won. So why are we still here?" https://www.washingtonpost.com/outlook/the-reformation-is-over-protestants-won-so-why-are-we-still-here/2017/10/26/71a2ad02-b831–11e7-be94-fabb0f1e9ffb_story.html?utm_term=.5e83a8e8e118.

Jerome, Jerome K. *Three Men in a Boat*. London: Penguin, 1994.

Käsemann, Ernst. *Commentary on Romans*. Translated by G. W. Bromiley. Grand Rapids, MI: Eerdmans, 1980.

Kilcrease, Jack and Erwin Lutzer, eds. *Martin Luther in His Own Words: Essential Writings of the Reformation*. Grand Rapids, MI: Baker, 2017.

Kreider, Tim. "The 'Busy' Trap." *New York Times* (June 30, 2012). https://opinionator.blogs.nytimes.com/2012/06/30/the-busy-trap/.

Lindsley, Art. "Priesthood of All Believers." Institute for Faith, Work, and Economics, 2013. https://tifwe.org/resource/the-priesthood-of-all-believers/.

Luther, Martin. "Avoiding the Doctrines of Men and a Reply to the Texts Cited in Defense of the Doctrines of Men." In *Word and Sacrament I* (*Luther's Works* 35), edited by E. Theodore Bachmann, 125–53. Translated by William A. Lambert. Philadelphia, PA: Fortress, 1960.

———. "A Brief Instruction on What to Look for and Expect in the Gospels." In *Word and Sacrament I* (*Luther's Works* 35), edited by E. Theodore Bachmann, 113–24. Translated by E. Theodore Bachmann. Philadelphia, PA: Fortress, 1960.

———. *Commentary on the Epistle to the Romans*. Translated by J. T. Mueller. Grand Rapids, MI: Kregel, 1954.

———. *The Epistles of St. Peter and St. Jude: Preached and Explained*. New York: Randolph, 1859.

———. *Galatians*. Crossway Classic Commentaries. Edited by Alister McGrath and J. I. Packer. Wheaton, IL: Crossway, 1998.

———. *Lectures on Genesis, Chapters 1–5*. In *Luther's Works* 1, edited by Jaroslav Pelikan. St. Louis, MO: Concordia, 1958.

———. "Martin Luther at the Diet of Worms." In *Career of the Reformer II* (*Luther's Works* 32), edited by George W. Forell, 101–

31. Translated by Roger A. Hornsby. Philadelphia, PA: Fortress, 1958.

——. "On the Councils and the Church." In *Church and Ministry III (Luther's Works* 41), edited by Eric W. Gritsch, 3–178. Translated by Charles M. Jacobs. Philadelphia, PA: Fortress, 1966.

——. *Preface to the Letter of St. Paul to the Romans.* 2 vols. Translated by Andrew Thornton. Munich: Roger, 1972.

——. "The Small Catechism." In *Martin Luther's Basic Theological Writings*, edited by Timothy F. Lull, 480. Minneapolis: Fortress, 1989.

MacDonald, George. *Unspoken Sermons.* New York: Cosimo, 2007.

Martyn, J. L. *Galatians.* The Anchor Bible Series, vol. 33A. New York: Doubleday, 1997.

——. *Theological Issues in the Letters of Paul.* Nashville, TN: Abingdon, 1997.

McGrath, Alister E. *Luther's Theology of the Cross: Martin Luther's Theological Breakthrough.* 2nd ed. Malden, MA: Wiley, 2011.

Sayers, Dorothy. *Creed or Chaos.* New York: Harcourt, 1949.

Smith, Christian, and Melinda Lundquist Denton. *Soul Searching: The Religious and Spiritual Lives of Emerging American Teenagers.* New York: Oxford University Press, 2005.

Voss, Hank. *The Priesthood of All Believers and the* Missio Dei. Eugene: Pickwick, 2016.

Watson, Duane, and Terrance Callan. *First and Second Peter.* Grand Rapids: Baker, 2012.

Wingren, Gustaf. *Luther on Vocation.* Evansville, IN: Ballast, 1994.

Contributors

Stephen Andrews
Principal of Wycliffe College

Robert Dean
Adjunct Professor of Theology

Terence Donaldson
Lord and Lady Coggan Professor of New Testament Studies

Alan L. Hayes
Bishops Frederick and Heber Wilkinson Professor of
Church History

L. Ann Jervis
Professor of New Testament

David Kupp
Professor of Pastoral Theology

Joseph Mangina
Professor of Systematic Theology

Judy Paulsen
Professor of Evangelism, Director of the Institute of Evangelism

Thomas P. Power
Adjunct Professor of Church History, Theological Librarian, and general editor of the Wycliffe Studies in Gospel, Church, and Culture series

Ephraim Radner
Professor of Historical Theology

Peter M. B. Robinson is the Professor of Proclamation, Worship, and Ministry and the editor of this volume.

Catherine Sider-Hamilton
Professor of New Testament